INSPIRING LIVES

REGGIE BUSH

Superstar on Offense

By John O'Day

I0892214

Gareth Stevens
Publishing

Please visit our Web site www.garethstevens.com. For a free color catalog of all our high-quality books, call toll free 1-800-542-2595 or fax 1-877-542-2596.

Library of Congress Cataloging-in-Publication Data

O'Day, John.
Reggie Bush : superstar on offense / John O'Day.
p. cm. — (Inspiring lives)
Includes index.
ISBN 978-1-4339-3647-0 (pbk.)
ISBN 978-1-4339-3648-7 (6-pack)
ISBN 978-1-4339-3646-3 (library binding)
1. Bush, Reggie, 1985—Juvenile literature. 2. Football players—United States—Biography—Juvenile literature. I. Title.
GV939.B836 2010
796.332092—dc22
[B]

2009037374

Published in 2010 by Gareth Stevens Publishing
111 East 14th Street, Suite 349
New York, NY 10003

Designer: Michael J. Flynn
Editor: Mary Ann Hoffman

Photo credits: Cover (Reggie Bush), p. 1 (Reggie Bush) © G. Newman Lowrance/Getty Images; cover (field), p. 1 (field) Shutterstock.com; p. 5 © Chris Graythen/Getty Images; p. 7 © Rick Stewart/Getty Images; p. 9 © Stephen Shugerman/Getty Images; pp. 11, 19 © Harry How/Getty Images; pp. 13, 15 © Jamie Squire/Getty Images; pp. 17, 27 © Tom Hauck/Getty Images; p. 21 © Donald Miralle/Getty Images; p. 23 © Lisa Blumenfeld/Getty Images; p. 25 © Stephen Chernin/Getty Images; p. 29 © Chris Trotman/Getty Images.

Printed in the United States of America

CPSIA compliance information: Batch #CW10GS: For further information contact Gareth Stevens, New York, New York at 1-800-542-2595.

Contents

Who Is Reggie Bush?

Reggie Bush plays football for the New Orleans Saints. His uniform is black, white, and gold.

SAINTS

Reggie runs very fast. He is good at catching and carrying the football.

25
SAINTS

Reggie was born in San Diego, California.
He was born on March 2, 1985.

Reggie's Family

Reggie was raised by his mother and stepfather. They like to go to his games.

SC
'06
PIONS
619
619
619

High School Sports

Reggie went to a high school with many students. He played football there.

Reggie could move quickly. He worked hard to become a good football player.

Reggie played other sports, too. He was a fast runner on the track team.

College Football

After high school, Reggie played football at a college in California. The team was named the Trojans.

Reggie was very good at carrying the ball.

He went around and over other players.

USC
5

Touchdown!

Reggie was very good at making touchdowns. He scored many points for his team.

A Big Award!

Reggie won an award called the Heisman Trophy in 2005. It is given to the best college football player.

Reggie wanted to play football all the time. He showed NFL scouts how strong and quick he was.

New Orleans Saints

Reggie joined the New Orleans Saints in 2006. He is one of the best players in the NFL.

06-50 S
1

Timeline

1985 Reggie is born in San Diego, California.

1999 Reggie begins playing high school sports.

2003 Reggie begins playing college football.

2005 Reggie receives the Heisman Trophy.

2006 Reggie joins the New Orleans Saints.

For More Information

Books:

Gibbons, Gail. *My Football Book.* New York: HarperCollins Publishers, 2000.

Pellowski, Michael J. *Football Facts.* New York: Sterling Publishing Co., Inc., 2007.

Stewart, Mark, and Mike Kennedy. *Touchdown: The Power and Precision of Football's Perfect Play.* Minneapolis, MN: Millbrook Press, 2009.

Web Sites:

NFL: Reggie Bush

www.nfl.com/players/reggiebush/profile?id=BUS294963

Yahoo Sports: Reggie Bush

sports.yahoo.com/nfl/players/7751

Publisher's note to educators and parents: Our editors have carefully reviewed these Web sites to ensure that they are suitable for students. Many Web sites change frequently, however, and we cannot guarantee that a site's future contents will continue to meet our high standards of quality and educational value. Be advised that students should be closely supervised whenever they access the Internet.

Glossary

award: a prize given to someone for doing something well
college: a school people attend after high school
NFL scout: a person who looks for players for the National Football League
touchdown: a six-point score made by carrying or passing the football into the end zone
track: sports like running, jumping, and throwing that take place on a running track and an open field
uniform: special clothing worn by members of a group or team

Index